EVOCATIVE INTERIORS

EVOCATIVE INTERIORS

RAY BOOTH

FOREWORD BY BOBBY McALPINE

RIZZOLI
NEW YORK

New York Paris London Milan

To my mother, Betty Booth, thank you for all you have invested in me—a love of nature,
an appreciation of hard work and a job well done, the meaning of home,
the belief that we choose daily whether to walk in the light or the dark,
and an unquenchable thirst for the pursuit of beauty and its deeper truths.

TABLE OF CONTENTS

FOREWORD
BY BOBBY McALPINE

To awaken and walk in these thoughts we are given to is a privilege as designers. But to grow over decades alongside the fierce intelligence and talents and joyful hearts of your chosen family is divine. It has turned my life into university.

My first encounter with Ray Booth was as a teacher and he a student of architecture. He shined above all others in his sensitivity, romantic point of view, and deft hand. New York bound, it would be ten years before he would become my partner in the firm now known as McALPINE.

Architecturally trained and interiors practiced, Ray's disciplined eye has made him a cut above. Listening closely, he has brought to the table a comprehensive, keen sensitivity and integrity that can be spotted in a millisecond in much the same way it shows in his person.

"Use me for good. Walk me in good company" is a little homemade prayer I recite to myself. Ray is indeed good company. The works of my life have often been graced by his thoughtful eye and touch. Many others here hold his sole vision. Distinct is his empathetic signature. Handsome, intuitive lines layer and build in subtle color and texture, hosted by large, quiet scale and gesture. There resides in his work a young spirit and an old soul netting a maturity and energy and timelessness to rooms that both hold and deliver you.

Kind, firm, curious, and playful, these designs celebrate all that is refined and polished by eclectic choice. The parts, though often opposites, have a knowingness of each other that perhaps they could not be better than for the other's presence. Like music, there are base, gravel tones and weightless, silky heights. Casual and elegant, these rooms have a voice you can live with, and they will last. There is a sense of safety in these rooms, made up of intelligent characters and strong movements.

Know it is my honor to share a name, a practice, and a lifelong friendship with Ray, as he continues to reach higher ground through the gorgeous invitations we receive. Thirty years in, it seems we have just begun to tap into the ether that carries the magical, curative qualities of home.

In this book are but a few of the people met along the way. Each introduction hones a new facet in the journey. Each of you exercises a different corner and asks the good questions. Can you see me? How do I look? What would you have for me? Inspired, these pages illustrate how Ray has walked a few of you home.

INTRODUCTION

From my earliest moments of awareness, I have known home to be meaningful, both as matter and metaphor. Our everyday surroundings are a mark we make to claim our place on earth. The daily experiences they evoke through the combination of color, material, furnishings, and context profoundly affect our physical and emotional well-being. Within the sheltering confines of floors, walls, doors, windows, and roof, far greater psychological intangibles of comfort, security, and belonging can and should exist.

Through interior design and architecture, we journey toward the realization of a soulful ideal, a lovely, lasting home expressive of our inner being. Only when we hear the language of our hearts can we seek, think about, and choose the best options for defining those worlds of beauty and peace of mind. Design of any kind begins with focused listening to elicit the who, what, and why of the given endeavor. The hope for beauty sufficient to capture and excite the imagination, and to not let it go, emerges more often than not from the intense conversations at the beginning of every undertaking. It may also be born out of the site itself, for one or more facts of place may be so specific as to direct the interiors and architecture to become what they should be, whether modern, traditional, or somewhere in between. Always, the particular why and who of the given design endeavor determine the what it is to become.

When I was a child, my mother and I would drive around my hometown of Huntsville, Alabama. One of our favorite routes took us through Huntsville's beautiful Twickenham Historic District. The pure grandeur of the architecture fascinated me. My mother's response saw beyond the beauty to the emotion. The antebellum homes suggested to her as much an inner state of happiness as an outward expression of wonder and the security implicit in the survival of structures standing their ground for generations. I began to absorb her sensibility.

As I grew, architecture gained its hold on me. Pencil, paper, brushes, and paints became tools for my forays into design. In high school, I kept on with drafting and art classes, my sketch pad always with me. Compelled by some as yet undefined creative urge, I spent nights at home fashioning houses on graph paper instead of doing homework. At Auburn University, all the wheels of a future in design started turning. There, I met two people who have inspired and encouraged me to this day: Bobby McAlpine, who eventually became my business partner, and David Braly, one of my first professors (and later my thesis advisor), who grew into a dear friend and works with us even now.

Auburn's curriculum was neither a classicist's type of education nor a modernist's. Although we learned the nuts and bolts of history, the continuum of periods and styles, and how to put things together, our studios emphasized search and discovery, and how to use the tools of the classicist to innovate for our own time. Interning in Bobby's office my last two years of school, I felt as if I'd arrived in some mystical place of inspiration and discovered an architecture of romantic, resonant expression through which I could channel my own creativity.

Our everyday surroundings are a mark we make to claim our place on earth.

Seeking farther horizons after graduation, three friends and I moved directly to New York City. Soon after arriving, I was fortunate enough to land a position in the office of the brilliantly talented John Saladino. Working in the architectural department there led to yet another type of awakening. As my eyes opened to the world of interior design, I began to learn just how deep, layered, and evolved home could become when created by someone gifted in using interior design's particular tools with an artist's sensibility.

From Saladino's office, I moved to Clodagh's firm, an entirely different study in thinking differently. Clodagh was, and remains, all innovation. Thrillingly, she has neither rules nor limits. Brilliantly, she reinvents textures and materials from the "old world." In the captivating new worlds that she creates, organic curves and shapes, not straight edges, define form and space.

As interior design continued to intoxicate me with its uniquely expressive power to reflect character and personality in the elements of place, I swerved closer toward it, always keeping architecture within my peripheral vision. It's been said you can't go home again. My experience shows you can, provided you return with a toolbox filled with new playbooks and tools. When Bobby McAlpine called in 1998 to offer a partnership position in his firm in Montgomery, Alabama, I had been in New York for a decade. As much as New York remained the city of my deepest dreams, I was looking for my next professional frontier. Returning to Montgomery pushed the edges of possibility, yet experience has taught me to view whatever may lie ahead from all directions, including the one opposite to where you think the answers will be.

As a partner at McAlpine, I have moved our offices from Montgomery to Nashville and expanded back to New York. Through this journey, I have been putting into practice what the language and significance of interior design has helped me to discover. En route, I have found myself on a quest to tap into design's fullest powers of expression. My design process has always depended on the deep involvement of my clients, in part because my goal for each of them is a uniquely reflective home expressive of their particular truths. Until recently, the worlds we have created together have been interior ones. In the last few years, architecture has come back into my focus. It is an unexpected and longed-for gift to be able to return to my roots in structure and construction with the insight accruing from decades of experience with interiors. To sit at a drafting board putting pencil to paper—seeking, thinking, choosing—is always a designer's perfect opportunity. To be afforded the luxury of forming and fine-tuning every aspect of a home, inside and out, to the last detail and nuance, uniquely for those who will inhabit it fully every day is a designer's ultimate challenge and happiest responsibility. Therein lies the possibility of realizing the evocative ideal—a home instilled with a reflection of the heart, made manifest in the surroundings.

PHILOSOPHY

TO SEEK

In design as in life, what is unseen often drives what is exposed in the light. Every home has an inherent subtext, a greater nature, along with the hard facts of its pragmatic material realities and functional necessities. The process of design seeks to find a marriage, or at least a commonality, between the two main components of each residence: the person and the place. Some types of houses, for example, are meant to be on a hilltop, wide open to the world beyond their walls, grateful to material reality, humble before nature's grandeur. Others, and often those in urban areas, require a focus oriented toward the comforts of more intimate confines. This meaning of place is but one place to start.

To understand what hits a person in the heart, to hear another's hopes and dreams—these guide my sense of design direction for every endeavor. All sorts of questions help me to elicit this information. Where and how did you meet? What gives you joy? What breaks your heart? In the happiest time you can remember being alone, what were you doing? What's the happiest you remember being as a couple? What is your definition of home? How do we discover what is meaningful to you in space? What will give us a foundation for growing this project? We all live our lives in phases, requiring different things at different times. The meaning of home must reflect these deeper truths because a home should endure for more than a short while.

The idea of endowing an individual dwelling with a panoply of human qualities, with a soul, may seem a philosophical leap too far. Yet this is what we strive for: spaces responding sensitively to all the quotidian aspects of the everyday, rooms exuding kindness and emotional balm.

The key to imbuing each residence with the essence of the individual lies in discovering what the psyche responds to most: which particular color(s) of the spectrum offers a caress, which individual materials and textures proffer companionship and compliment, which piece(s) of furniture prompts an intriguing conversation with another piece of furniture. These relationships spark the elements of the emerging story of place and person. Each selection, every choice, influences the other. Slowly, selections with significance and resonance emerge. The specifics of each space are born out of this process. Often, they get worked out in the doing.

PAGE 2: Bringing a Palm Beach interior into balance, light plays off dark, curved off straight, and antique off contemporary. PAGE 5: Throughout our Nashville house, nature commands the view and light wields its magic. PAGE 6: In terms of forms, colors, materials, and the art of placement, a tabletop tableau mimics an interior landscape in microcosm. PAGE 9: A two-story space inherently requires layering and scale for comfort and intimacy. PAGE 14: Treated as art, a composition of handmade mirrors creates impact on entry. OPPOSITE: For authenticity, all the antiques in this Cape Dutch house have a pedigree from northern Europe.

The process of design seeks to find a marriage, or at least a commonality, between the two main components of each residence: the person and the place.

There is an art to the placement of things, a certain "rightness" of organization and proximity we all seek to create or impose on our environments. A minor adjustment of an angle, an alteration of half an inch—from the miniscule comes the mighty. The smallest moves can prompt in us an exhalation of breath, an inner feeling of energized calm telling us we have achieved what should be so. The specific details of what absolutely fits in a particular design are not always explainable by the underlying logic of form and function. In the quest to find the just-right arrangement of roof and windows to wall, of seating to table, of accessories on a surface, of colors and textures together, intuition inevitably comes into play. The dominant factor fueling the design of a home made uniquely bespoke for its occupants may be a palette of colors or materials, sense of place, or style. Whether the catalyst happens to be art, a trip, an emotion, or a deeply felt memory of place, the only way to discover it is by asking enough questions and spending enough time until it comes to the surface, unfurls its secrets, and exercises its magnetic force.

Discovering what creature comforts matter most, expanding them in the joyful possibilities of our day-to-day life at home, these are the ever-evolving, endlessly mysterious parameters of interior design and architecture. The seeking is ongoing. The wondering is vigilant. All the senses should be on high alert, open to possibility, always. Experience accrues and insight sharpens over time. Earnest, determined pursuit leads to the realization of one of life's great revelations and joys. There is always more to learn and additional options to try in the effort to discover, through design, the better nature of home.

PAGES 18-19: Enhanced proportions and modern materials transformed this room's existing fireplace into a focal point. OPPOSITE: The library's existing mahogany ceiling called out for a color palette and materials of equal depth and richness. PAGES 22-23: When a room lacks the luxury of wall space for artwork, we search for opportunities to integrate it in other ways.

There is an art to the placement of things that we all seek to create or impose on our environments. A minor adjustment of an angle, an alteration of half an inch— from the miniscule comes the mighty.

OPPOSITE: In a small room on the garden's edge, backing a sofa into the window bay made spatial and emotional sense. Mid-century chairs by Edward Wormley mix with a classic English table. PAGES 26-27: Bobby McAlpine and David Baker, two of my architecture partners, devised the berths that match the gabled end of a Cape Dutch house. We created a hanging fixture to echo the gable line.

TO THINK

Interiors and architecture with personal meaning always come into being through a process of critical thinking.

The first phase of each and every design undertaking centers on the search to discover as much as possible about the "who" of the project. The second phase, programming, explores the public and private ways we live within our houses, and the spaces our various daily activities require. This is when drawing as an analytical skill enters the picture. Yes, the act of putting pencil to paper is a form of alchemy, in its way. In design, drawing is where art meets thought, simultaneously a method of exploring and communicating ideas and a pathway for the conveyance of meaning.

For a from-the-ground-up house, a down-to-the-studs renovation, or a substantial addition, sketching general bubble diagrams helps to determine proper spatial adjacencies and flow. For an endeavor involving interiors only, the initial phase serves as a form of space planning, a kind of urban design for the community of rooms within the structure. Once it becomes clear which area pertains to what purpose, it becomes possible to decide the kind and assortment of furnishings to best serve the functional necessities.

Subsequent routes of design exploration follow from a subsequent series of questions: How does the mix of pieces most comfortably organize and arrange itself in the particular volume in terms of proportions and heights? Where will the sitting happen? What direction will the sitters face? What will each one see? How does any particular seated posture support what is the greater truth of the surroundings? The near, middle, and far views should acknowledge a sense of place, the material realities of its interior and exterior landscape, playing to what's already there. The design must attend thoughtfully to the practical details of living and the various activities occurring within the space. Through all these questions, any nascent inklings about color palette and/or material selection begin to come into focus.

Philosophically and aesthetically, this process of reasoning distills down to a search for a particular, personal hook on which to hang the design. By definition, it is different in every case. Yet, commonalities exist. Whatever is innate to the site or the larger context may act as a contributing factor(s). The emotional makeup and preferences of the specific people involved do as well. And if the house already exists, inevitably there will be a range of pragmatic responses to the environment in its current state. There may also be an art collection, preferred views to capture, a color palette, or some other particular feature of the person or the place suggesting itself as

OPPOSITE: To take a Federal-era house in Baltimore into its fourth century, we integrated modern elements of blackened steel (references to the Inner Harbor area's industrial buildings) with surviving colonial traces. PAGES 30-31: The captivating world beyond the windows is the focus of my Nashville living room.

A designer must be open to the possibilities of change and evolution, allow for discovery and chance, and welcome circumstances happening of their own volition. Flexibility, inspiration, and intuition inevitably find their way into a disciplined analytical process.

fastener for the many strands of the decision-making process. The challenge is to coax all the seeds of information gleaned, pearls of impressions gathered by dint of the search, inchoate longings felt, and thoughts expressed about what is most important into an organic, conversational, and physical logic ruling the rest of the choices. By virtue of this process, the creation becomes rooted in either the family or the site.

Planning is an intellectual exercise and essential to a successful design. "Fortunate" accident is just as important to a happy outcome. A designer must be open to the possibilities of change and evolution, allow for discovery and chance, and welcome circumstances happening of their own volition. Flexibility, inspiration, and intuition inevitably find their way into a disciplined analytical process. Often the best-laid plans, most clearly realized dreams, and most clever of schemes end for naught at the time of installation, when it becomes absolutely clear how the room will benefit by spinning all components around and repositioning them in places where they were not originally intended to be. The need to see critically and consider decisions from various different perspectives are intrinsic to the process of creativity.

Design is a learned lesson in the power of dichotomy and the connectivity of nuances spanning polar opposites, a parable, of sorts, in built form. Through all the shades of dark we come to know the subtleties and moods of light. Through all the forms of modern we begin to comprehend the antique. Perhaps more importantly, through an understanding of the past we reinterpret the now. Everywhere we look, we see opposites in abundance: organic versus man-made, permanent as opposed to perishable, stately against relaxed. Endless fascination lies in the possibilities of each joint and juncture, in the practicalities of every mechanical and emotional connection, for these reveal the magic of hope and opportunity manifested in material form. Only through deep thinking (and its companion, seeking) do all-important distinguishing degrees of difference reveal themselves.

OPPOSITE: In this house, the back sides of opposing fireplaces create a powerful architecture of entry. Papier-mâché frames—one with a mirror, one without— enhance the drama. PAGES 34-35: In an Alabama house by my architecture partners Bobby McAlpine and Greg Tankersley, contemporary furnishings in neutral tones heighten the effect of the gutsy, traditional surroundings.

OPPOSITE: At one end of a Baltimore dining room, contemporary seating around a fireplace provides a gracious gathering spot for before and after a meal. ABOVE: At the other end of the same dining room, an upholstered screen embraces another seating area. We created the paneled walls and ceiling beams to echo the history of the Federal-era house, then departed from the past with our furniture selections.

RIGHT: Sometimes, we all need something a little unexpected—like, in this case, the Kelly Wearstler wallpaper that brings much-needed animation to the smallest, darkest room in our house, a guest room under the deck.

In design, drawing is where
art meets thought,
simultaneously a method
of exploring and communicating
ideas and a pathway for
the conveyance of meaning.

TO CHOOSE

Life has its rhythms. So do interiors and architecture. They are by definition far more fixed in space and time. What do you do when you first wake up? Where do you go to do it? What type of space should it be? What emotional needs are met there? Does the family eat together? Where in the house do they gather to dine? At what time? Is there always a fire in the fireplace? We all have rituals we employ as we go through our days. It is important not only to discover what those customs and ceremonies are for each family and every house, but also the preferences involved in the particulars of how a person and a family choose to bathe, dress, cook, dine, entertain, sleep, and so on. Such information enriches the ability to select and arrange the components of each space so the rituals occurring therein can evolve into their ideal expression. These kinds of choices are not only the dictates of the creative process; they are also what enhance the actual experience of life within the home.

Our daily ceremonies happen in and through our individual spaces, in moments of passage and rest, in color palettes, textile selections, and furniture options. A beat, a pattern, a transition from light to dark, from cozy to expansive, from glass to plaster, from steel to wood to stone, from soft to hard, can excite the soul of those who engage every day with a structure and its interior. The body reacts viscerally to material, texture, volume, and plan. The particular relationships of ceiling, wall, and floor; of door and passageway, of window and roof; and of the furnishings within the built frame: all factor into the physical and emotional impact of a given place.

Context is the first principle of design above all, both in the large and small details of the interior landscape, its color and materials palette, and in any aspects of the surrounding interior architecture and exterior structure. My preference is always to relate the inside to the outside, to try to construct an interior truth with powerfully honest, authentic components, fascinating in their simplicity. I am open to any material and color palette harboring a connection to the place where it finds itself. (Blackened steel, graphite, plaster, quartzite, limestone, masonry, linen, leather, glass, and wood are personal favorites.) The selections speak to far more than mere decorative pleasure. There must be visual delight. At best, these types of choices connect the design to a context in the heart. When they do, they anchor themselves securely in the different emotional needs to which every home should attend. When they do, the harmonies resonate.

Light is the magic elixir in any successful design, whether interior landscape or architectural surrounding. Doled out in small measures, light can and will endow whatever it falls upon with the ineffable grace of its presence. When it pours into a room abundantly, it bathes

OPPOSITE: In a family room, we like to incorporate seating with different postures and personalities. The room's color palette takes inspiration from the gardens just outside the windows. PAGES 46-47: In the renovation of this residence, we enlarged the living room by incorporating space from an adjacent study.

The particular relationships of ceiling, wall, and floor; of door and passageway, of window and roof; and of the furnishings within the built frame: all factor into the physical and emotional impact of a given place.

everything in its purview with its liquid luxury. Part of nature's own, ever-changing drama, light shifts from hour to hour, day to day, season to season, year in and year out. Every house should celebrate the sun's organic rhythm in the choreography of its rooms as they step from airy, happy, and bright to smaller, more intimate, all-embracing confines.

Too much of even a good thing can be mundane. We all crave the feeling of integrity attending to an interior and a structure constructed with clear, concise logic and sharply focused aesthetic. All of us, too, reach a longed-for moment when the element of surprise, of an unexpected gesture, brings us home. First we must establish rules. Then when opportunity calls, we must choose to break them.

The essential facts of habitation have evolved over centuries into the far richer experience of residence we know so well now. From the earliest days of human civilization, our dwellings have been a special mark we humans make to claim our place on earth. Shelter is safety and what we seek from our first breath. Even more, it connects us to family, community, state, country, and era—all the layers of our personal world as we think them to be. Today, home is a place of refuge, a necessary restorative, a space for companionship, an environment for personal growth—and, yes, the portal we come to for the choices of our creative expression.

OPPOSITE: For more intimate dining, a lower table (twenty-six to twenty-seven inches high) surrounded by lounge seating presents a European flavor. PAGES 50-51: In today's expansive interiors, we strive to ensure that the proportions of the upholstery respond correctly to the grandeur of the architecture. PAGES 52-53: In our New York apartment, the painting over the sofa worked its wonders in three ways: as a pop of color, as inspiration for the room's palette, and as a point of interest to draw the eye.

First we must establish rules.
Then when opportunity calls,
we must choose to break them.

PROJECTS

TIME AND AGAIN

Sometimes in design one has to step back in time in order to move forward. This Nashville couple took this trajectory when they decided to move from the gracious, French Mediterranean house created for them by my architect partner Bobby McAlpine, where they had raised their family. With their teenagers rapidly approaching young adulthood, they opted for a great stone beauty dating to the 1930s for their next phase of life. She toured Bobby through the house. Working with Chris Tippett, another of our partners, Bobby encouraged them to carry out the idea of an addition with a larger kitchen. At this point, my office took over the interior architecture, interior design, and furnishing. The challenges were numerous. Chief among them was recasting the more intimate rooms typical of the house's era into the light-filled, airy expanses we prefer to live in today. No less important was determining a more contemporary yet timeless style of decor best suited to the family, who had long dwelled in a traditional environment graced with a collection of beautiful antiques.

The reinvention happened in phases, with construction coming first. Much of the interior's original decorative woodwork had survived through the years in its original finish. These beams, moldings, bases, mantels, overdoors, and casings factored significantly into the charm of the spaces, but their oaky coloration (prevalent in the 1930s) created a visual heaviness contrary to the spirit of this quintessentially gracious couple. Painting all the woodwork the same color as the walls reintegrated the details into the architecture, creating understated textural definition and intriguing sculptural profiles.

Our goal was to find a way to edit the interior architecture without destroying the house's traditional character. Belgian-inspired design provided the inspiration for the more contemporary language we were seeking. After stripping much of the woodwork, we painted the remainder an off-white, chalky shade to match the walls. This unified the interior vistas and transformed the decorative woodwork into a kind of shadow play, quietly activating the rooms with subtle silhouettes and surface texture.

Before we moved them in with their existing furnishings, we combed through all of their pieces deciding which to keep and where to introduce some new items. She and I took a shopping excursion to New York, where we found a few choice designs, though more modern than antique. One in particular, a large, square coffee table from the 1960s, became a launching pad for all the decisions to come. With a black laminate top (measuring just shy of sixty inches by sixty inches) on a clear Lucite base, the coffee table took on a dual role: as an offering place for the display of some of her treasured accessories, from antique bookstands to books, and as a centering device for the dance of the sofas and chairs.

Two years of transformation and editing later, the house came to reflect the richness of their personalities and the enduring warmth of their hospitality. As such, it was an unusual amalgam of past lives and projects, but one no longer speaking to one specific moment in time.

PAGE 56: Beauty, simplicity, and scale are the animating spirits of this stair where an oversized (and very unexpected) antique wood urn creates interest atop a steel plinth. OPPOSITE: Of sufficient scale and proportion, the statue of the monk is perfectly placed to draw the eye as a focal point of the living room.

ABOVE: To simplify this interior and quiet it down, we removed an existing fireplace mantel, pared away architectural detail, and painted all the woodwork the same color as the walls and ceiling. OPPOSITE: An oversized, 1960s-era laminate tabletop found while shopping with the client in New York acts as a modern center of gravity in a room filled largely with the clients' existing antiques.

ABOVE: Wrapping the one-time dining room with a raffia wallcovering, we reinvented it as an intimate family lounge. OPPOSITE: Drapery can do more than frame windows. Here it softens the room, increases its emotional warmth, and gathers its objects together. PAGE 64: Converting a library to a dining room, we opened up the back wall with a glass door system to connect it to the pavilion beyond. PAGE 65: Perfect for the family's antique book collection, the dining room's existing built-ins also offer opportunities for the display of art.

PAGES 66-67: My colleague Chris Tippett's thatched roof pavilion unifies this house's outdoor living spaces. RIGHT: Glassed in on two sides, this kitchen has very little wall space for the usual countertops and appliances. The two islands—one for prep, the other for cooking—provide all the necessary function.

RIGHT: Bigger is not always better.
This family of five often gathers
for meals around the bistro-size table
in the keeping room off the kitchen.

RIGHT: An upholstered screen embraces the bed and
nightstands. Low enough to hang art above it, it also does
double duty as a headboard. Banking the drapery on
either side adds another layer of texture and design interest.

MODERN FAMILY

Family culture and architectural context have always factored heavily into my design point of view. With longtime clients such as these restaurateurs, the cumulative effect of collaborative experiences has enriched those insights. These bore fruit in their triplex in one of the Upper West Side's iconic, early twentieth-century grand dames, the fifth (and largest) residence we've done together. Ample enough for the growing family's needs, it also offered them yet another opportunity to realize their dream kitchen: a professional, stainless-steel–clad temple to the culinary arts with a distinctly residential overlay for entertaining gatherings of extended family and friends. By the time we began planning the three-floor home, they had already determined the kitchen and dining areas would occupy the top floor because it had the highest ceilings and terraces for outdoor dining, socializing, and lounging.

These clients wanted a modern vision for this project. The contextual challenge was to develop an interpretive expression of the style and materials of the building's exterior and the drumbeat of detail in its memorable Art Deco lobby through a full-on contemporary lens. Reeded and fluted details served the purpose, translating into visual and literal texture on paneled walls, doors, and cabinetry. Strong, simple materials such as rift-cut and quarter-sawn oak echoed throughout the residence as a unifying theme. A stair traversing all three floors was an opportunity to create a serious piece of interior architecture, a wonderful boon. Inspired by the premise of deconstructed Art Deco, it incorporated square bronze panels to frame each piece of glass, with industrial-age connections and mounts to hold the different spindles, all wrapping into a beautiful, little rounded newel post at each end.

The large salon, bathed in buoyant southern sun, was a bit of a design poser as it lacked any kind of focal device, such as a fireplace. For a visual anchor, we devised a deep niche framed and cased in a rich, darkly stained eucalyptus wood. A custom floating cabinet with a stone top and fluted door details introduced a sense of scale. To add to the layered effect, we descended a series of thick, bronze bar stock trapezes from the ceiling as mounts for two-inch-thick Lucite shelves for vases, sculptures, and books. Organized groupings of custom upholstered seating and bespoke tables (some responding to the building lobby's Art Deco aesthetic) ranged within the niche's gravitational pull.

Because the family had begun to collect, we wanted the fabric palette to allow the artworks full due. Textiles and carpets hovered in the neutral zone of off-whites, grays, and beiges, with some pops of color and intriguing textures to animate the space. In the family lounge, we opted for upholstered walls and dark fabrics to mask any wear from active young children.

Here, the family's present and future and the building's past factored deeply into the materials and choices of design. As a result, the residence was bound to reflect the uniqueness of their personality and place.

OPPOSITE: Vintage ceiling pendants in the entry hall
of this New York triplex echo the lustrous bronze,
steel, and glass railing that unifies the three floors.

PAGES 76-77: In the living room, a neutral palette in rich textures offers visual interest yet allows Ron Gorchov's *A Night in Tunisia* to take center stage. The furnishings mix contemporary and period pieces with an echo of Deco. RIGHT: At the living room's opposite end, the built-in bookcase created a focal point for a room that had been lacking one. The open-frame sofa allows light to spill through the structure.

ABOVE: Antonio Lupi's solid stone sink adds sculptural functionality to the powder room. RIGHT: In the dining room's sitting area, custom étagères of steel and wood provide verticality. On the wall, a work by Blair Thurman provides focus. PAGE 82: The client's dream restaurant-style kitchen incorporates custom steel cabinets, stainless-steel base cabinets, and a walnut eating surface. PAGE 83: The coffee bar's design derives from a tansu chest in my Nashville home.

RIGHT: On the west side of the
residence, the master bedroom takes
its color palette from the city's
magical, pink-tinged golden sunsets.
Hanging over her desk is
Diana Al-Hadid's *Secret Sisters*.

OPPOSITE: A chaise in the master bedroom takes in the cityscape. THIS PAGE, TOP: Her crisply tailored dressing room features cabinetry of rift-cut and quarter-sawn oak. RIGHT: A freestanding tub from Lefroy Brooks anchors their capacious master bath. PAGE 88: Custom, his-and-hers chaises are perfect for intimate tête-à-têtes beneath the Anish Kapoor prints. PAGE 89: The walls of the family media room are upholstered in a sound-absorbing heavy wool. Holton Rower's *Untitled* adds jolts of color over the sectional.

CHANGE AGENTS

Transformation requires both vision and courage. When the change involves a complete about-face in homes and interior aesthetics, there's often a clear catalyst. For these clients, a young family of five (plus two cats and two dogs), the impetus was inadequate display space for an expanding collection of art and mostly contemporary photography (by Sante D'Orazio, David LaChapelle, and Sally Mann, among others). Having outgrown their much-loved, traditionally elegant Southern home, they started searching for something more: a warm, welcoming, modernist exemplar appropriate for their family life, their art and photography holdings, and entertaining of all kinds, from philanthropic events to family gatherings.

What they found was the perfect starting point: a hilltop perch of seventeen wooded acres overlooking the Nashville skyline, with an existing house from the 1990s. Large, L-shaped, and chunky, with low ceilings and few windows, the residence didn't quite meet their needs. It was, however, blessed with great basics: generously proportioned living, formal dining, and other areas for entertaining massed at the front of the house along a bisecting hallway, with the family living quarters in two stories at the rear.

With architects from the Nashville firm DAAD, we reimagined the structure's every facet and surface into an art-accommodating, sleek-yet-warm modernist composition of limestone and glass embracing the natural world all around. Peeling off sections of the original entry (housed in an octagonal tower) allowed us to fashion a new, formal, gallery-like entry in what was the original living room. Removing selected floors created the soaring expanses required for their large light sculptures. To ensure every room offered ample opportunities for art display, we invented flexible hanging devices and integrated them into every wall surface imaginable. Raising the central corridor's ceiling from ten feet to twenty-four feet and marking its endpoint with a floor-to-ceiling window recalibrated the artery's purpose from functional passageway to gallery space for their larger holdings, such as Martin Schoeller's portrait of Angelina Jolie. To knit the interiors to the exterior, we wrapped the master suite with a courtyard and terrace, extended a spacious porch off the grand, formal living room, and refined the pool area and lounge adjacent to the kitchen and family dining spaces.

Imbuing the surroundings with palpable warmth are textural, emotionally evocative materials including stone floors, stone walls, and wood ceilings, all in subdued hues selected to show the art to best advantage. As a softening gesture, limestone walls divided by an integrated steel lintel received different finishes on the upper (sandblasted) and lower (bush-hammered) planes. Hand-scraped, wood-paneled doors brought in a human touch. To layer in contemporary style and classic comfort, we mixed modern and vintage furnishings dressed in organic shades of creams and browns, restful, watery blues, and soft, lichen-greens. Arresting pendant fixtures artfully filigree the volumes overhead.

For this family and this house only a complete transformation would do. It occurred thanks to their vision and courage—and the life-altering power of their art.

OPPOSITE: We wanted to open the house up to the views with as much glass as possible. Many of our design decisions—including removing an upstairs library to create a two-story space for their U-Ram Choe light sculpture—revolved around finding ways to accommodate their collections. In spaces as dramatic as this living room, we'll often look for furnishings with a low center of gravity that appear to reach out to the floor.

RIGHT: With a very monochromatic palette, it's critical to play to either end of the spectrum with deep, dark notes and light, airy shades. The steel I-beam that bisects the fireplace wall is both a visual enticement and a practical device for hanging art. Two different finishing treatments animate the wall's stone surface: above the beam, the stone is sandblasted for softness; below, it's bushhammered for texture and the play of light.

RIGHT: We refashioned the original living room into a more gracious, immediately welcoming entry gallery by including inviting furnishings as well as the family's art. Contrasting with the strength of the architecture, the dangling bubble chandelier is an element of surprise. PAGE 96: Beyond the entry, a limestone cube becomes a backdrop for a custom hanging console; the black channels facilitate the hanging of art and the flow of air. PAGE 97: Banked draperies incorporate softness into the architecture. We wanted to include an anomaly, breaking the rules of the room for creative tension, hence the antique Spanish theater chair.

RIGHT: The central axis dividing the interior looks back toward the family's everyday entry. Overhead, a suspended graphite cube creates a play of volumes and helps direct the placement of the art, including Martin Schoeller's close-up photograph of Angelina Jolie.

ABOVE: In the powder room, walls lacquered a shade between eggplant and chocolate create drama; with its scraped surface, the door introduces a touch of the hand. OPPOSITE: The kitchen's steel island precisely mimics the dimensions of the skylight. PAGES 102-103: We pulled the soft hues of the master bedroom's palette from the private garden beyond. PAGES 104-105: The loggia was our solution to the clients' request for a multifunctional outdoor room.

MOUNTAIN MAGIC

In days gone by, and always with exceptions, each region of our country had its own recognizable design style. A certain look tended to prevail in the mountains, at the beach, in urban areas, and so on, with thematic variations on the norms at play in the north, south, east, and west. These comfortable, predictable forms of beauty have given way for the most part to the individuality of our age. When clients know their own minds, aren't afraid to be different in their decor, and have the courage of their design convictions, the collaboration involved in creating a home takes on a special energy. These Nashville-based clients exemplify this type of boldness. They called us in just after they purchased a vacation home at the Yellowstone Club in Montana. While the exterior was complete, the interior architecture was just taking shape. The timing gave us an opportunity to work with the architect to refine the detailing.

Typically, every interior in the Rockies, Grand Tetons, and other points west of the Mississippi told the same Big Sky Country design story: hefty rustic beams, massive stone fireplace, antlers everywhere, and all tied together with oversized furnishings and iconic Western paraphernalia. The pair of them wanted anything but. Because they intended to display some key works from their collection of modern and pop art (among them one of Robert Indiana's numeric sculptures and an Andy Warhol self-portrait), they actually needed the interiors to be clean and modern.

Set on a sloped site, the two-story house took its planning cues and flow from the topography. The main floor was the center of the action for the prime public and private areas: living room, dining room, kitchen, master suite, office, and back porch. A full lower level housed another lounge, children's rooms, and guest rooms.

By paring back and simplifying all the applied architectural elements and finishes (wood-paneled ceilings, beam work, stonework, door casings, doors, and moldings), it was possible to transform what had been envisioned originally as a rugged, rustic, mountain setting into the urbane, contemporary background for art and living desired by the clients. From a decorating standpoint, the airy, light-filled rooms asked for a comparable glow of creamy shades and blond tones. Contrasting dark wood accents; aged, patinated, and blackened metals; and some selective dashes of strong color added the necessary gravitas with style.

For furnishings, we mixed antiques among the contemporary pieces, with upholstered seating taking cues from traditional forms. Textiles ranging from hide to linen to cashmere introduced a subtle but complex layering of textural heft and sensuality. Some cozier, darker spaces provide emotional rhythm and contrast, among them the stone-lined entry salon to the master suite and an espresso-walled nest of the family room—the most unexpected, and fun, of all.

OPPOSITE: In seeking the right balance of context, style, and personality for this mountain home, we pared back the obvious Western elements while still incorporating materials, forms, and details appropriate to the place.

RIGHT: The entry introduces the unique contrast of rustic and refined. A collection of antique industrial rings fitted with mirrors and chairs by André Arbus break up the expanse of stone. PAGES 110-111: Oversized sofas face off in the living room. The clients' sound sculpture anchors a corner of the room. A Damien Hirst piece is a target for the eye on the fireplace mantel. PAGE 112: Drapery serves as a layering device for framing rooms within rooms. The top of the dining table is wood from a former dance floor. PAGE 113: We kept the kitchen's traditional elements and simplified the details to give the room a more contemporary look. A large, very long island serves as its functional centerpiece.

RIGHT: The volume of the master bedroom asked for a canopy bed and embracing draperies to introduce a sense of architecture, scale, and intimacy. We pulled the snow-white palette from the winter landscape; the dark browns, from the bark of the trees.

RIGHT: Dramatic and dark, the sitting room is a chic nesting place with Robert Indiana's sculptural number 2 and, over the sofa, a Warhol. Perforated leather draperies diffuse the light. A thick Tibetan carpet lays a foundation of pattern and texture.

HOUSTON MODERN

For those with an adventuresome streak and an eye refined for design and decoration, change has proved to spark creativity, and, occasionally, unexpected domestic choices. When this active family of five relocated from their expansive, traditional house in Savannah, we helped them renovate a mid-century modern box in Houston, where inspiration didn't just strike, it galvanized.

Completely captivating to the wife, the daughter of an interior designer who inherited many of her mother's talents, the house of choice surprised me on first viewing. A flat-roofed relic of 1961, about half the size of today's homes, it contained the small, low-ceilinged rooms standard to the era. She knew if we gave the living spaces the love they needed, the family could easily pare back and live within the house's original footprint as happily as in their much larger Savannah home.

Apart from white paint, a few lanterns, and shutters to veil the master suite's street-facing windows, the exterior stayed true to its origins. Its original interiors were also intact, replete with dark wood paneling, Harvest Gold appliances, and other period elements. Our renovation focused on opening up all the rooms to the light and the landscape while subtly invoking visual continuity with the house's past.

In the foyer, a metal screen with panels of rippled, amber glass still stood guard. Using the existing framework, we replaced the 1960s aesthetic with a modern, louvered structure serving the same organizational purpose, punctuating the division between the stair on one side and the dining room on the other. Inserting a two-story window opposite the stair and unifying the flooring on the main level with white concrete pavers (except in the master bedroom) created a sense of spatial enlargement and enhanced the dance of light throughout.

A Sheetrock ceiling and constrained fireplace marred the main living space. Expanding the fireplace surround with a horizontal mantel and flanking steel panels restored the significance of its gestural impact on the room. Planking the ceiling with poplar similarly added character and a timely reference to vintage style.

The original kitchen was tiny, with a pantry and a mudroom off to the side. Combining all three into one expansive work space, we installed a wall of windows over the stove, centered a skylight over the kitchen island, and secreted most of the storage behind full-height, paneled doors.

She furnished the rooms, with some consultation and collaboration from me. A few choice pieces nodded to her mother, who always advised: "There needs to be some brown wood." An antique linen press, top removed, standing proud on a custom steel mount, provided the signature glossy brown touch. More important, it introduced a bit of personal history, reinvented to suit the spirit of this reinvented house.

OPPOSITE: To transform the original screen at the entry into a more contemporary idiom, we switched out its amber glass pieces for bronze-colored slats. A custom limestone top updates her antique bench, a longtime family possession.

ABOVE: In recoloring the exterior of the house and refining its details, we added operable shutters to unify the front facade and offer privacy to street-facing rooms on both floors. The custom lanterns are my own design. OPPOSITE: A walled side garden presented an opportunity to layer the living space into the exterior. PAGES 122-123: A planked ceiling adds texture and interest overhead. A natural interior designer with a great eye, my client selected and arranged all the furnishings, art, and accessories (with some consultation on my part).

OPPOSITE: The original living room fireplace was a timid gesture. We extended it horizontally to give it the strength it needed, flanking the firebox with patinated steel panels, and added a simple limestone mantel.
THIS PAGE, TOP: An antique linen press mounted on a custom steel base becomes an unexpectedly contemporary expression of traditional brown wood furniture.
RIGHT: Her collections adorn the coffee table.

PAGE 126: Dining room seating doesn't always have to match. It can be much more fun and interesting to bring different personalities to the party. The room called out for a piece of jewelry, hence the chandelier. PAGE 127: In rooms with only one window (like this dining room), a mirror activates the space by bounding around light and views. RIGHT: To open up the kitchen, we annexed the mudroom and pantry and then installed horizontal aluminum windows to capture the garden view. A Frank Thiel photograph adds a punctuating note.

CHANGING WITH THE TIDE

Many of us revel in each and every opportunity for transformation, at home and elsewhere. Such has been delightfully the case for this New York family, longtime clients who have taken great pleasure in exploring different facets of their design identity with each successive residence we've created together.

When the couple purchased this well-built but fairly unremarkable two-story beachside residence, we had already collaborated on two city homes: the first, a chic SoHo loft; the second, a traditional Upper West Side townhouse. This getaway had all the benefits of the shore location in its favor. It needed refreshing, however, and the couple wanted to take its interiors in a novel direction. They envisioned this home as a gathering place for the large groups of friends and family whom they regularly entertain with beautifully prepared lunches and dinners. As a result, the kitchen became a primary focus. From the outset, they elaborated their overall goals for the design clearly, mandating a crisper, more contemporary palette of materials and furnishings reflective of the simplicity of beach life.

The first time I went out to see the house, it was one of those misty beach mornings, all soft, purple-blue hazes and ethereal, wispy tones. There was our palette: shades of soft grays meandering through the rooms like a whisper. The front door opened to a large, two-story entry hall, which felt oddly uncomfortable and too typically suburban. Building a second floor overhead not only brought the volume back to human scale but also created an upstairs lounge for the children.

The living room occupied the front of the house, as did a closed, separate dining room with access to the poolside area. Since we knew they would spend their time from dawn to dusk in this exterior space, it hardly made sense to have the rooms designated for evening use and focused on what would be more or less invisible views. Moving the living room toward the back of the house and opening it up to the dining and lounging spaces instituted a much better flow and more practical arrangement for the daily life of the house. Planking the ceilings here, as well as in the kitchen and the upstairs master suite, introduced an embrace of much-needed warmth and distinctive character. Replacing the fireplace surrounds with simpler, more architectural frames transported the rooms into a much more modern mode.

In the kitchen, a sleek minimalism prevailed: simple, flush finger grooves, surfaces of Luce de Luna quartzite (a personal favorite of mine), and a range hood sprayed with glossy automobile paint. The bathrooms received a similar reimagining, with planked walls, smart contemporary fixtures, and floating vanities.

A series of material and decorative interventions helped transform the upstairs master bedroom from a blank Sheetrock expanse into an airy, beachside refuge. The upstairs children's lounge was made to serve more than one purpose: when curtained off, it can do double duty as a bunkroom for sleepovers with friends.

As transformations go, this one was top to bottom, inside and out. A newly polished facet of the clients' design persona, it gleams with their modern spirit.

OPPOSITE: Combing out this interior's more suburban materials, we introduced soft linens, smart cottons, and driftwood-like planking on the ceiling to create an ethereal, beach-inspired environment. Sheer linen curtains filter the light. A white hide rug adds texture underfoot.

OPPOSITE: In our redesign, we switched the dining room and the living room bringing the dining room closer to the light and view (the living room we moved away from light since it is used at night for lounging and TV watching). The coffee tables add a playful, salty punch of black that enhances a predominately white palette. THIS PAGE, TOP: Antique ship's pulleys introduce a nautical touch to the hanging console that anchors one side of the living room. RIGHT: A hammered silver lamp base and strings of shells on metal dowels add hints of luster.

RIGHT: An island of Luce de Luna quartzite centers the kitchen. To keep the open feeling, we used exposed shelves instead of installing upper cabinetry. A custom steel étagère holds cookbooks and cookware. PAGE 136: To escape all the Sheetrock in the master bath, we lined the walls with flush planked shiplap. PAGE 137: In the lofty, vaulted sitting room off the master bedroom, a fireplace redone with a black steel surround and beveled limestone mantel provides a quietly dramatic focus.

RIGHT: The master bedroom offers a crow's-nest view of the ocean and pool below. Gauzy linen sheers at the windows filter the light in a palpably transporting way.

PAGE 140: To bring the original two-story entry back to human scale, we laid in a ceiling and added a simple railing and bannister.

PAGE 141: On the stair's upper landing, built-in window bunks can double as extra sleeping space for overflow, with a privacy drape that stretches from wall to wall.

PAGES 142-143: The outdoor living room is a perfect spot for cocktails.

TRAVELER'S RIDGE

My inner architect has always longed to design, construct, and furnish a home from the foundation up, a yearning realized in Traveler's Ridge, our hilltop house overlooking Nashville. It took two years to nurture it from conception to fruition. The process allowed me to test and temper my evolving ideas about what makes a house a home and to meld our individual tastes and preferences into a unified vision.

We'd purchased the lot almost on a whim, and certainly on my husband's love and trust. Though I'd enthused to John about its beauties and possibilities (at the end of a cul-de-sac, no immediate neighbors), I'd made clear its potential drawbacks (charred ruins of the previous house would have to be removed) since he was unable to visit the site before the take-it-or-leave-it deadline.

We split our time between Nashville and New York, so a smaller footprint contained within the existing foundation felt appropriate, especially knowing we would extend our living space into the landscape with expansive terraces and gardens. Our original dream dwelt on a modern, flat-roofed farmhouse. The power of context prevailed: because Traveler's Ridge would be visible from every conceivable vantage point, a hipped roof (a reference to the hill's parabola) felt more organic. Masonry with one glassy box bay window to offer welcome gave the street-facing side the necessary privacy. Inside, the masonry gave way to a glass facade overlooking Nashville and threw open its arms to the endless vistas.

From a programming perspective, it made sense to house guest suites and a lounge for visiting family and friends on the lower level, public living spaces on the entry level, and a roost for ourselves on the top floor. We also gave ourselves private perches to work and several more-contained areas for nesting.

The furniture plans came first, as they must, even with architecture. How else could we ascertain whether the activities and flow between seating, dining, cooking, and resting supported the house's greater truth? Here, the view was the dominant fact. Every aspect of the interiors, including a color palette echoing the purple blues of the distant mountains and the whites and silvers of the clouds, paid homage to nature's surrounding beauty.

Over the years, experience has taught me an important lesson about many spaces considered mundane. They should be treated as anything but. Dressing rooms, closets, baths, and other hardworking everyday areas can affect the ease of our daily rituals profoundly. In the master suite, we incorporated a tub and a shower oriented toward the view. Both guest suites and the guest lounge made the indoor/outdoor connection apparent with access to adjoining terraces. And because of our tiny New York closets, we were comparatively extravagant in our dressing room and storage here.

I have always told my clients how a house, when it's right, can encourage us to become our best selves. At Traveler's Ridge, the life-enhancing lesson came home.

OPPOSITE: The cathedral window creates a lofty yet welcoming
entry and channels daylight as it pours into the interior.

RIGHT: The landscape suggested the form of the house and its palette of exterior materials. The brick seems to melt directly into the surroundings. Dark muntins and mullions echo the trunks of the trees in coloration and verticality. The step-backs allow the structure to reach out to the site below. PAGES 148-149: The screen becomes a layering device that heightens the surprise of the transition between entry and living room. Steel accents provide necessary structural reinforcement. The palette of whites, grays, and silvers takes its cues from the clouds.

LEFT: The entry door is integrated into the wall of cathedral windows; chamfered limestone details add definition and depth. OPPOSITE: On the other side of our living room fireplace, our evening room offers a cozy place to read. Auvie and Roust, our Siamese cat twins, love to cuddle up there, too. PAGES 152-153: Like an island, the rug defines the dining room within the larger context of the open plan. We blew out the corners of the house with glass for a more expansive view. PAGE 154: Decks and terraces extend the living spaces of the house into the landscape. PAGE 155: Building within the foundations of the previous (and larger) house offered an opportunity to create a uniquely layered, indoor/outdoor experience.

RIGHT: In the kitchen, a metallic graphite backsplash reflects light from the front of the house. The custom range hood combines a few of my favorite materials: rift-cut and quarter-sawn oak and steel. An antique tansu provides linen storage. PAGE 158: A working pantry offers convenience on the other side of the range wall. PAGE 159: The powder room's graphite walls and a counter of reclaimed barn wood are rustic notes that tether it to Tennessee. PAGES 160-161: Meant to be a floating, loft-like response to the power of the hill, our master bedroom looks down as much as it does out and up. A railing provides a vertical connection to the living room below.

159

ABOVE: Our dressing room has been a lesson for us in the importance of daily rituals, like getting ready for a party or packing for a trip, and the roles they play in making memories. OPPOSITE: The doors of the master bath open to a terrace with a glass railing. To bring in as much natural light as we could and from as many angles as possible, I installed skylights over the vanities.

RIGHT: A wardrobe in one of our guest baths has been an interesting exploration of using furniture in place of built-ins. PAGES 166-167: In the adjoining bedroom, my tête-à-tête bed allows the guest to choose not just the side of the bed, but also the preferred view.

A DELICATE BALANCE

When couples have differing aesthetic sensibilities, design can become a process for marrying the two. His eye appreciated the very formal and traditional. Hers gravitated to the more modern, casual, and Asian-inspired (from a childhood spent in the Far East). It may have seemed as if the twain would never meet, but ultimately they did.

The two had come to Bobby McAlpine, my architecture partner, to create their next Nashville house and invited us to do the interiors. With their children grown, they wanted a residence supportive of gracious entertaining for gatherings large and small, which would also allow them the privacy to live entirely on one level. An elegant, fluid, loft-like, open-plan sequencing of public spaces from the front of the house to the master suite at the rear met our goal. Massive wood columns on either side of back-to-back fireplaces helped differentiate the various volumes from receiving to dining to a family room. Beyond the trio of airy welcoming areas, a little sunroom beckoned, with kitchen and butler's pantry on the far side of the axial hallway processing to the master suite. The upstairs was given over to three en-suite guest rooms and a lounge; the basement, to additional guest and recreation areas.

To get the design of their interiors underway, they visited my Nashville home, Traveler's Ridge, to discuss their aesthetic goals. She in particular felt at home there, but was articulate about wanting their spaces to have a more feminine twist. A shopping trip to New York offered insight into how to bridge the gap of their differences in preferred styles. As we visited showrooms and antiques dealers, we saw furnishings, lighting, and accessories in both the modern and traditional camps. When it became clear how the various designs could balance each other out, we began to find their common aesthetic ground.

In the entry, for example, a fine French commode nodded to his appreciation of the classic, while happily sharing the spotlight with several of her Asian treasures. In the family room, a contemporary curved sofa made a sweeping statement by the window, yet within glancing distance, an antique dining table provided a fixture of tradition. In the light-washed master suite, a modern Murano chandelier descends tantalizingly over a quintessentially contemporary freestanding tub.

Peppering an array of blue tones through the various areas paid homage to her favorite color—a palette as a unifying thread. Those hues found echoes in the mirrored overdoors, which were chemically treated to remove most of the silvering off the mirror back, leaving just the minutest bit of reflectivity in a beautifully abstract, textured, and colored surface.

The disparate components of their mix ultimately melded into a unified sensibility. The elegance born of his love of formality and tradition, coupled with her preference for the modern and casual, as well as treasures from her youth, created a uniquely personal aesthetic—and a home expressive of them both.

OPPOSITE: The receiving room of this Nashville residence melds the couple's different aesthetics. The antique propeller table standing sentry at the center of the room infuses the lofty space with a spirit of tradition. The blackened steel racks stacked with wood evince a contrasting taste for the more modern and organic. PAGES 170-171: My partner, Bobby McAlpine, designed the house, which presents a welcoming face to the street. Interestingly, the proper front door to the house is actually along the side.

ABOVE: An antique chest in the entry hall becomes an opportunity to display some of her Asian treasures. OPPOSITE: The playful, graceful line of the stair inspired the trio of lanterns dancing at different heights. We designed the niche for her statue with an appropriately shaped arch.

RIGHT: A tall screen upholstered in linen serves as both a gathering device and a backdrop for a mix of contemporary furnishings and antique pieces collected over a lifetime. The settee is one of my own designs.

RIGHT: In the family room, we looked for opportunities to combine large contemporary gestures such as the curved sectional with more traditional, smaller-scale flourishes. In the overdoor at the entry to the adjacent sunroom, antique mirrors with the mirror finish etched away add subtle reflections and an iridescent shimmer; the abstract surface introduced hues that we incorporated into the color palette of both spaces. PAGES 178-179: On an axis with the sunroom entrance, a fireplace wall anchors the opposite wall of the family room. The contrast in wood tones and colorations heightens the happy tension between the rustic and the refined.

RIGHT: Painting the sunroom a dark brown was a conscious decision to direct the eye to look to the light and appreciate the landscape. Across the hall from the kitchen, this room becomes a keeping room while she's cooking for family and friends. The swivel chair is a great place for relaxing with a glass of wine during preparations for a meal.

OPPOSITE: In the master bath, we sited the freestanding tub to take advantage of the view. A Murano glass chandelier adds a note of modern glamour overhead. ABOVE: Wrapping the master bedroom in a pale lilac grass cloth helped to soften the space and make it more feminine. A sculptured, upholstered headboard allows them to read comfortably in bed.

TEXAS STATE OF MIND

Design almost always emerges from the nexus of necessity, invention, and context. This Texas-born family returning from Washington, D.C., to Austin's rolling hills, experienced a similar truth. After a protracted search, they purchased a large, two-story, redbrick house with a black slate roof. While the 1980s structure met their imperatives for size and location, it was wanting in every other way. In its need for complete change, it offered us everything in the way of opportunity.

Taking the house down to the studs, we left only its roof, framing, and foundation intact. This skeletal structure yielded us the proverbial blank slate for architectural reimagining. To create much-needed rhythm and shadow play along the street-side facade, we introduced details such as glass box bay windows and clad the entirety in a rough-cut, in-state-quarried Lueders limestone. To instill an appropriate sense of arrival, we constructed an Italianate loggia at the front entry. To open up the rear to a new, large pergola (Austin has a comparatively temperate climate) and the scene-stealing view, we opted for ten-foot-high steel-framed doors and windows.

As found, the entry hall presented a two-story, and rather unwelcoming, conundrum: twin pageant stairs curved up to second-floor bedrooms kept separate by an unbridgeable gap. Laying in a floor helped to establish a more gracious, human-scale greeting by reducing the volume to one story. Installing a spiral stair to a newly created children's lounge and inserting a mezzanine to traverse the gap finessed those problems.

A similar architectural fix, a long mezzanine, corrected related problems of scale and proportion in the awkward transition between the entry and double-height salon. The additional layer of space also established a more intimate area around which to congregate elements of the salon's two seating groups. Because these clients wanted their family and friends to always feel at home, they requested comfortable, Texas-sized upholstered furniture, which we coupled with the best of the antiques from their Washington home. Her preferred palette of creams and light grays gave the entire house a lightness of being.

In a pair of existing single-story wings, we installed a sleek family kitchen and an oak-paneled library. These adjustments spun the floor plan around, yielding an exceptionally large, formal dining room in space vacated by the original kitchen and family room, which the clients wanted to be able to transform for gatherings of different types and sizes. Centering the dining table, installing ancillary seating areas to hug up against the windows, positioning a small table by the fireplace, and hanging a movable drapery "wall" to partition the room as desired accomplished the goal.

The master suite remained along the front facade. To imbue the room with character and redoubled purpose, we introduced a favorite antique screen, curved sofa for a window seat, and small Sheraton desk.

Through reimagining, this house has become a home: a place tethered both to its context and to this family.

OPPOSITE: The original entry of this house featured a two-story front hall with twin stairs that didn't connect the rooms on the upper level. We laid in a ceiling with plaster detail to restore a sense of human scale, and replaced the two stairs with one beautiful, sweeping spiral.

RIGHT: Supports for a mezzanine that we layered into the living room (see pages 190-191) and pairs of Tuscan columns establish a sense of procession and an architecture of entry through the public spaces of the house. Custom, ten-foot-high steel and glass doors open the back of the living room to a furnished terrace and the views of Austin's rolling hills beyond.

ABOVE: A very contemporary Murano glass chandelier injects a strong, modern note into the architecture's classical bias. OPPOSITE: Large-scale furnishings suit the proportions of the room and ensure comfort for family gatherings. The wingback chair is a custom design. PAGES 190-191: A space as large as this can be a challenge to furnish. We opted for two seating groups, each with its own character. At the far end is a music salon organized around the grand piano. Opposite it is a gathering spot for TV watching and more casual family occasions. Antiques from the clients' former home in Washington, D.C., also made the move to Texas.

PAGE 192: When antiques contrast with more contemporary pieces, like the upholstered swivel chair and the marquetry table, the challenge is to find the most harmonious balance among the different elements. PAGE 193: We turned a long hallway between the kitchen and the dining room into a gallery by lining it with custom vitrines filled with her collection of Depression glass. RIGHT: The dining room's extremely ample dimensions allowed for seating groups of various sizes: a long, formal table arrangement at the room's core; an intimate table for two by the hearth; and a matched pair of round tables for four (or six) in twin window bays. The coffers overhead add depth and dimension that help tame the volume. A custom mirror by the window reflects light into the room's heart.

RIGHT: The whole
family gathers in the
library at the end of
the day to spend
time together,
whether working,
doing homework, or
just hanging out.
A custom, extra-long
library table offers
space to spread
out for two or more.
The lamps and steel
bookshelves are
also custom designs.
The entire room
is paneled in rift-cut,
quarter-sawn oak.

RIGHT: To create functional storage without resorting to the usual built-in cabinets, we developed this vitrine for glassware. It marks the entry to the kitchen and stands diagonally opposite its sibling version that displays her Depression glass. PAGES 200-201: The family kitchen is multifunctional, incorporating several options for dining, as well as comfortable seating for family members and friends to gather around while food preparation is underway.

RIGHT: In the family entry on the other side of the house, an arched ceiling adds interest. An English table anchors the space; striped gauze draperies introduce a linear accent. PAGE 204: In the master bedroom, a curved sofa fits into the box bay window we added to the front of the house. PAGE 205: Behind the bed, drapery serves as a centering device. PAGES 206-207: Texas-quarried Lueders limestone replaces the original red brick to finish a redesigned facade articulated with an Italianate limestone loggia flanked by symmetrical box bays.

RIGHT: A columned loggia on the rear of the house extends the living space into the landscape, cutting the harsh southern sun that had previously roared into the living room. The clapboard-clad rear wings break up the vista with a layering of materials.

MEETING POINTS

When marriage partners hail from different cities or states, there are all sorts of logistics to resolve, design-related and otherwise. Each member comes into the union with particular aesthetic biases and style preferences, and geographic ones as well. In this way, proximity to the places we love becomes intrinsic to the map of future family life. These clients charted such a course, hailing from different points along the Eastern Seaboard. She, a native New Yorker, and he, a born and bred Baltimorean, planned to make their family life in Baltimore. To stay closely connected to her New York–centric family and friends, they looked northward for a summer house, purchasing Treetops, a historic, nineteenth-century property in Southampton, famed for its glorious gardens.

The house was just as one would expect: a romantic, cedar-shingle-clad rambler with great charm, a little bit of sag here and there, beautiful but not too perfect. In other words, it needed work. The challenge was to find a way to respect the historic nature of the original interior architecture with its bold beamed ceilings, paneled walls, and wainscoting while bringing the rooms into the twenty-first century to suit their young family lifestyle. The renovations happened in phases. First came a new kitchen and keeping room (in space appropriated from a neighboring area). A year-and-a-half later, the bathrooms received an overhaul.

In this rich setting, truly traditional decor would have felt too formal and heavy for a summer getaway. Yet an ultra-modern approach with cutting-edge style would have been inappropriate. To create the right timeless spirit, we opted for clean-lined, transitional furnishings with carefully chosen antiques—some Italian pieces along with light, elegant, painted Swedish Gustavian designs—peppered in here and there. Fresh, crisp, slipcovered sofas and lounge seating provided the casual elegance along with the hoped-for comforts. But what truly gave these interiors their contemporary sensibility was the surprise of size. In the smaller rooms attending to an older house like this, ordinarily the sofa of choice would be seven and a half feet. We decided to do otherwise and went large with nine-foot sofas—gestures of scale endowing these spaces with the visual texture of our times.

For the fabrics, the natural choices were linens and cottons, the typical textiles of summer. They tend toward soft shades of blues and greens in a palette that takes cues from the garden to tie interior and exterior together. In the family room, we pushed the color story a little further, adding in bursts of oranges and other accents related to the hues of the flowers right outside the windows.

Until now, this historic house has reflected the family ties binding this couple's first years together. Now with two young children and some history of their own, they're set to reinvent parts of it all over again.

OPPOSITE: The palette in the master bedroom picks up hues directly from elements of the Hamptons' landscape and the gardens surrounding the house.

RIGHT: Working within the context of this historic house, it was important to find ways to make it comfortable for a family with young children while still respecting the integrity of its proud architecture and the rather intimate dimensions of its rooms. PAGES 214-215: Had the furniture plan for this living room followed the lead of the ceiling beams and other rectilinear elements, the end result would have felt very constricting. Shifting the focus off the orthogonal to the diagonal and angling the individual pieces give the room a breath of fresh air. It also makes the most of the view of the garden just outside the French doors.

ABOVE: The clients entertain frequently and wanted the dining room to be as flexible as possible. The inclusion of two tables—one round, one long—on either side of the room's central axis helps achieve the objective. OPPOSITE: The round table fits neatly into a bowed window bay. PAGES 218-219: A historic house contains many opportunities to weave in furnishings of various personalities and periods that may not seem necessarily "right" or expected, but that bring the spirit of the house into the present. In the family room, mid-century modern chairs and a modern bronze coffee table surprise, but they infuse the mix with the tenor of the times.

LEFT: The new kitchen responds to the age of the house in its details, and nods to a more contemporary aesthetic with open shelves and storage designed to resemble furniture rather than cabinetry. PAGE 222: An existing bookcase opposite a bay window framed a perfect spot to place a game table for family gatherings. PAGE 223: To open up the master bedroom under the eaves, we removed some built-in vertical cabinets.

RIGHT: A glassed-in porch presented itself as the perfect setting for family dining. We nested a banquette and table into the corner to allow a comfortable perch on the edge of the garden. The large windows slide open, allowing the aromas of the garden to waft through the space.

SOUTHERN CHARMS

The architecture of a house may seem almost magically apt when its gracious spirit feels as if it mirrors its owners' generosity of heart and mind. These Baton Rouge–based clients found their perfect architectural match early on in their family life when they succumbed to the remarkable charms of the work of architect A. Hays Town (1903–2005), a designer of resonance renowned for memorable houses in his home state of Louisiana and elsewhere throughout the South.

The couple had commissioned Town to design their first house, the homestead where they raised their family. Through the years, as architectural fans, they had always admired this French-and Creole-inflected house (one of Town's finest) with its beautiful interior courtyard sequence. When it came on the market, they purchased it from the original owners, who had not updated it since its completion around 1980. Our challenge was to alter it enough to accommodate the clients' contemporary lifestyle while respecting, without being bound to, all of Mr. Town's principal design gestures.

Town cast his design spell with a mix of character, authenticity, and historical precedents. His handsome, contextually specific residences often incorporated reclaimed and repurposed materials. Here, he integrated numerous elements with the patina of history into rooms redolent with references to Louisiana's multicultural past. Because the flow of the house felt organic and right for the place, the climate, and these clients, we left the floor plan essentially intact. We also retained his very rustic finish on the beams, enriched the coloration of the heart pine floors, and repainted the walls in a cool, light gray. One of our few, minor architectural adjustments involved recasting the main living room's existing fireplace in a softer, less attention-seeking mode. Removing its original brick columns and mantel and straightening out the angled flue to create a simpler, square plaster fire front accomplished our purpose. The effect of these changes allowed us to reorient the seating groups around the large windows to face the sunlit courtyard and to provide a gracious welcome from the front door.

This couple had an interesting take on past and present. Their furnishings reflected their different inclinations, balancing his taste for the more clean-lined and modern with her love of antiques. Combing through their existing collection, we assessed which pieces would look their best in these updated rooms. Then we combined those selections with roomy, clean-lined upholstered seating and other more modern pieces throughout. The mix refreshed the character of both the antiques and the upholstery and helped transform the much-admired house into a well-loved and lived-in home to reflect its new owners' personalities, not just Town's original vision.

Like other Louisianans I have met, this couple has lived each day with love, pride, and respect for their local culture and architectural history. In this house, they wanted their reverence for Town's ethic and aesthetic to shine through a more modern lens. It does.

OPPOSITE: A well-placed modern mirror in the entry of this house reflects on the history of this residence by architect A. Hays Town and the soulful effect of his use of reclaimed materials.

RIGHT: Sometimes it's necessary to look at the design of a room from a point of view exactly opposite to the usual. Simplifying the fireplace in the living room reduced its gravitational pull and allowed us to turn the furniture plan around 180 degrees to focus on the garden opposite it.

228

OPPOSITE: I love to layer different types of function into a dining room, hence my frequent use of banquettes along with other types of seating. The situation here offers options for everything from an intimate, elegant dinner party to a casual, quiet time reading the newspaper and having a coffee. ABOVE: Devising ways to integrate their existing antique pieces, including the dining room mirror and chandelier with our more contemporary selections, made us think very carefully about line, proportion, scale, form, and ornament.

ABOVE: One of the great charms of this house is its courtyard plan, which creates a beautiful enfilade of interior and exterior spaces. OPPOSITE: In a library off the living room, a warm palette with dark accents establishes a contemplative mood. Found on a trip to New Orleans, the chandelier incorporates antique bayonets. PAGE 234: Charlie looks out to the courtyard. PAGE 235: Oversized antique botanicals draw the eye through the interior enfilade. Playful rope ottomans are perfect for visiting grandchildren. PAGES 236-237: An upholstered screen embraces the bed, providing a visual anchor.

THE POWERS OF REFLECTION

For a client with a discerning eye and a well-defined purpose, a project may come quickly into sharp focus. This client, for example, treasured all things beautiful, above all, his wife. He wanted to build a home to honor her and pay homage to her utter loveliness. This family retreat on the shores of Skaneateles Lake in New York's Finger Lakes region, created with Boston-based architect John I. Meyer atop the foundations of the site's original 1902 house, emerged out of his wonderfully romantic directive.

Visiting the site for the first time just after dawn proved a transcendent experience. The surroundings were visceral in their beauty. As I marveled at the clarity of the light and colors, the sun's early morning rays reflected off the rippling water, launching magical, refracted beams dancing overhead. The icy blues, soft greens, and other hues innate to the site provided immediate cues for palettes and patterns.

Even before construction began, it was clear the front door should open to a spectacularly framed view of the glacier-formed lake. A central, three-story hall acknowledging the floor plan of the original house could then provide a grand entrance and organizing principle for the main level's living spaces. The second floor would be devoted to the master suite and other bedrooms. Because the client had envisioned a place always alive with guests, the top floor would become their private retreat.

His taste for formality influenced every last nuance of interior architecture and decor. A plaster ceiling, patterned to suggest my first, breathtaking experience of the dancing light, energized the entry with additional drama. Every surface received similarly attentive treatment, from the paneling to the patterned marble floors to the grand walnut stair.

Instead of sequestering away a formal dining room, we designed the entry hall to adapt to the purpose. Outfitted with a Regency-style pedestal table and lightly gilded, white-painted chairs, it provided a grand stage for the theater of entertaining at the table. For intimacy in the ample rooms adjoining it, we installed floor-to-ceiling curtains and embraced various sofas with low upholstered screens.

As a young man, the client had amassed a museum-worthy collection of nineteenth-century cobalt-decorated American stoneware and opened Manhattan's well-regarded American Folk Art Gallery (long shuttered). His knowledge and appreciation of art and antiques led us to pursue pieces at auction and through every antique dealer of merit in New York and Los Angeles. Artist and colleague David Braly, whose work the client had admired in another of our projects, sketched an enchanting mural of local flora, fauna, and specific lakeside sites. While the artwork was underway, the couple had a daughter, Clover. David added a final flourish, integrating a clover into the mural for love and luck.

When this client commissioned us, he was as clear as Skaneateles Lake about the kind of beauty beyond imagining he wanted to create—and why. I've experienced no better catalyst for design.

OPPOSITE: We lacquered the ceiling of this hallway to capture the drama of the dance of refracted light off the surface of the lake. Pulling the dining room out from behind closed doors into this space allows the table to do double duty as a center hall table, welcoming all with a floral tribute. The swath of the custom marble floor sweeps from the entry to the lakeside window.

RIGHT: The front door opens to a dramatic, three-story entry hall, carefully scaled and detailed with elements of interior architecture, including the paneling and the stair. Light floods into the space from several angles and heights. This client has an eye for antiques, so we searched the world for the best of the best. Attributed to the Sicilian architect Giacomo Amato, the pair of gilded consoles dates to the first half of the eighteenth century. PAGES 242-243: A mural by David Braly, a longtime friend and colleague, rings this casually elegant sitting room and the adjacent living room. High wainscoting envelops the interior, instilling a sense of scale and history. My initial view of the waves skimming across the surface of the lake inspired the plaster ceiling detail. PAGES 244-245: The formal living room contains more icy blues; the sitting room, more soft greens. Italian gilt-wood sconces stand at attention by the fireplace, with David's mural above.

RIGHT: In the library off the main entry, paint embedded with graphite gives the walls a voluptuous burnish and shine. The contrasting camel tones of the room enhance the effect and seem made to show off the honeyed woods of the Biedermeier chairs. Contributing to the masculine rigor are dark flannel draperies with the tracery of a windowpane plaid.

247

RIGHT: Pewter countertops suit this kitchen's traditional cabinetry. A planked ceiling lessens the formality. The adjacent family dining area is octagonal, which led us to put all the furniture (and the ceiling beams) on the diagonal. PAGES 250-251: In the master bedroom and sitting room, a steel four-poster bed acts as emotional architecture, creating an area of intimacy within the expansive volume. The upholstered screen serves a similar purpose. PAGES 252-253: The antique, L-shaped settees on the screened porch face captivating views in both directions.

ACKNOWLEDGMENTS

What a long and abundant list of people I want to thank for their faith and trust in me, and their encouragement. This work exists in large part due to them.

Bobby McAlpine, I am forever grateful for the inspiration you have instilled in me, your invitation to walk with you in this work, and the restraint with which you allowed me to find my own way while never abandoning me in any need or advice I sought.

I have never had a greater understanding of true intimacy until it was defined in daily, formerly inconceivable ways by my husband, John Shea. Thank you for the confidence and affirmation you continually offer me and for being the bedrock on which we have been able to build a beautiful and blessed life.

The richest of dreamers exist in my studio. Each of you is an integral part of the foundation of our work, which we are fortunate enough to explore on behalf of those who walk in our door. But you are beyond dreamers: you are catalysts of action, grace, and determination in the everyday. Thank you to Liz Thompson, Lindsay Griffy, Meredith Lovell, John Anderson, Jackie Collition, Erin Cypress, Eli Groman, Emily Richardson, Perrin Tyner, Caroline McDonald, Jennifer Lineberger, Molly White, Cathy Crowl, and LeeAnne Billen.

To the talented, loyal, and soulful makers, my other partners of McAlpine, in whose hearts and work I continue to find wonder and constant invention: Greg Tankersley, Susan Ferrier, Chris Tippett, John Sease, and David Baker, I am grateful for the daily commitment you each have to the service of our clients and the creation of our shared and individual work. Beyond my partners, there is the larger McAlpine family in offices in Montgomery, Atlanta, Nashville, and New York, too many to name. I believe we rise to the level of the great talent around us. You all continually raise that level in your work and inspire the rest of us to strive to do the same.

To each of our wildly talented craftsmen and craftswomen who have worked for years to realize our designs in upholstery, fine woodwork and furniture making, fine cabinetry, draperies, wall coverings, metalwork, and construction: Thank you for your constant hard work. Your efforts bring the shine to ours. None of this could be done without you.

So many editors and publications have cast their eye toward the work here, even in the earliest of days. I thank you all for your support and for the work you do daily to fuel the interest in this industry and the creative process of architecture and design.

There are champions whom we encounter every day. Among the greatest of these are those who see things in us that we might not acknowledge in ourselves. Jill Cohen and Judith Nasatir were among my champions in this endeavor. Thank you for seeing, listening, and encouraging the creation of this book; thanks to you both, I can say, "I am HERE!" Also, thank you to the photographers whose critical eye and compositions have eloquently captured the work: Eric Piasecki, Pieter Estersohn, Simon Upton, Laura Resen, Tria Giovan, Melanie Acevedo, Juan Pont Lezica, and Jean Allsopp. Thank you, Richard Norris, for lending your meticulous eye and deft skills as a stylist. Doug Turshen and Steve Turner, you have melded all these endeavors into a beautiful graphic interpretation. Also a deep thanks to Charles Miers of Rizzoli for taking a chance on me and to Sandy Gilbert, our editor, who ensured that all the parts became a comprehensible whole.

Lastly, it is important to me to note that none of this work would exist without those seekers who find us in their journey to realize homes that reflect their innermost being. To make such an investment employs courage and exposes the most private thoughts and desires. By this trust and faith from you, our extraordinary clients, I am humbled and continually thrilled. I am grateful for the role you each offer us in your search for the evocative home.

PHOTOGRAPHY CREDITS

Melanie Acevedo: 49
Jean Allsopp: 5, 146–147, 150
Pieter Estersohn: 16, 26–27, 30–31, 38–39, 91, 94–95, 97, 98–117, 145, 148–149, 151–167, 239–253
Tria Giovan: 2, 6, 42–43, 46–47, 92–93, 96
Juan Pont Lezica: 10
Eric Piasecki: 9, 13–14, 18–25, 28, 36–37, 40–41, 52–89, 169–209, 227–237
Laura Resen: 119–129
Simon Upton: 32–35, 45, 50–51, 131–143, 211–225

First published in the United States of America in 2018
by Rizzoli International Publications, Inc.
300 Park Avenue South
New York, New York 10010
www.rizzoliusa.com

2018 2019 2020 2021 / 10 9 8 7 6 5 4 3 2 1

Printed in China

ISBN 13: 978-0-8478-6188-0

Library of Congress Control Number: 2017956530

Project Editor: Sandra Gilbert Freidus

Editorial assistance provided by Deborah Gardner, Sara Pozefsky,
Rachel Selekman, and Elizabeth Smith

Art Direction: Doug Turshen with Steve Turner

Production: Susan Lynch